*O*rigami as presently conceived is about *line*, about lines and planes and flaps and layers and points, and in terms of process, about narrowings and stretchings and bringings of flap edges to a center line and sinking and tucking and collapsing and pulling open.

This other origami is about surface: a beautiful, clean, modulated surface, *uninterrupted* by hard folds as far as possible, and barely touched. Process is almost nonexistent considered in one way and almost endless when you consider the potential for shaping and the need for it. The main thing is to be able to look at that surface with the feature that is just starting to emerge, say a nose or a mouth (or just an abstract curve), and feel a wash of affection at its incipience. Whatever is done afterward is worthless if that incipience is lost. Mountains of technique, an infinity of steps—all very well—but if you can't preserve the innocence, what have you done?

SCULPTURAL ORIGAMI

Innovative Models, Plus a Gallery of the Artist's Work

SAADYA

DOVER PUBLICATIONS, INC.

MINEOLA, NEW YORK

Bibliographical Note
Sculptural Origami: Innovative Models, Plus a Gallery of the Artist's Work is a new work,
first published by Dover Publications, Inc., in 2011. A bonus instructional DVD has been included in this edition.

Library of Congress Cataloging-in-Publication Data
Sternberg, Saadya.
    Sculptural origami : innovative models, plus a gallery of the artist's
work / Saadya Sternberg.
        p. cm.
    ISBN-13: 978-0-486-47840-1 (pbk.)
    ISBN-10: 0-486-47840-8 (pbk.)
    1. Origami. I. Title.
    TT870.S7276 2010
    736'.982—dc22   2010025794

Manufactured in the United States by Courier Corporation
47840801
www.doverpublications.com

FOREWORD

What Makes Origami Special?

It is from *paper*. Crisp, dry, thin, colorful—associated with gift wrapping and gift giving—or perhaps plain brown or white, as widely available and unaristocratic as a material can be. All that origami needs in addition to paper is—intelligence.

It is from paper, *folded*. The creases are where the intelligence comes in: where mind impregnates paper. Invariably, a geometry of some kind appears in the sheet, starting in the (usually) square initial shape and continuing through each of the developing model's permutations of form. The sequence of folds itself can be natural or artificial, logical or whimsical, formally repetitive or full of its own rhythm and surprise. Typically, the poetry of a fold-sequence is reflected in the final object. Yet it is not only a geometric intelligence or a poetic sequence which is preserved in the end result; each individual folder's personality is reflected there too, like a signature, in the impress of that maker's hand upon the paper. Force, gentleness, bravado, timidity, thoughtfulness, obsessive repetition, or the grand flourish—all these qualities of character can come across in a piece of folded paper. For paper is the most receptive of the materials human art has known.

It is from folded paper, *uncut and unglued*. These limitations are crucial. They force the mind to find solutions. They keep the art, in all its diverse moves and stratagems, a single game, as chess is. They preserve the integrity of the continuous sheet, and so respect the value of chastity, the mystery and potential of the uncut membrane. They allow each final result to be reversed, unfolded if necessary all the way back to the flat square. This reversibility makes evident the unity or common paternity of all the different objects of origami, but also adds to the sense of the entire enterprise as a game, as intelligent play. For no fateful incisions have been made,

and no permanent bondings that can't be undone. Each step can, in principle, be taken back, or handled a bit differently. This adds to the freedom or freshness which shines from the works.

A paper-fold sequence *can be taught*. Origami is fundamentally a communicative art. Objects are typically designed so others can make them. Whereas in most of the plastic arts it is every man for himself, in origami things are more like in music: a nice design will be "performed" by many people besides the "composer." Interpretation is encouraged. Feedback is quick and from multiple sources, so the art as a whole rapidly improves. Also as in music, origami designs can be communicated both face-to-face and indirectly, through graphic diagrams which are comparable to musical scores. This dual-transmissibility, which is recent (the standard notation for diagramming origami moves was settled on only in the past sixty years) has led to an explosion in the number of new origami models and to their rapid internationalization. The latest designs by hot creators quickly hop across the globe, a process sped up even more now by the Internet. Conventions are held every year in dozens of countries, in which hundreds of folding enthusiasts show off their productions and eagerly share tips and techniques.

What makes origami special? This question is being asked by museum directors as well of late. Increasingly in recent years, large-scale exhibitions of origami art have been held in leading venues around the world—the Peabody-Essex Museum near Boston; the Tikotin Museum of Japanese Art in Haifa; the Pendulum Gallery in Vancouver; Hangar-7 in Salzburg; the Mingei Museum in San Diego; the Louvre in Paris; and the History Center of Zaragoza. Invariably in these venues there is surprise at the vastly increased attendance these shows bring, and the enthusiasm of the visitors. All age groups and social classes seem to be drawn. Why is origami successful when other contemporary arts sometimes fail? Well, origami really *is* different. Contemporary it may be (most of its leading practitioners are alive today), but it is not anti-traditional, as it holds a deep respect for its centuries-old origins. Nor does it view handicraft with irony or disdain, for it itself is the most "handy" of crafts, nothing coming between the maker's fingers and the sculpture being formed. It does not dwell on the chaos of modern life, but chooses to expend its intellect on the considerable problem of getting a good goldfish from a square. It can have nothing to do with the big name artist, his inflated ego or prices—for what it cares about is ordinary paper, and through it, the connection with ordinary people. And this is what draws the crowds. For all origami does, is make a little magical something out of almost nothing. It is *still* "just a sheet of paper"—but now with enough genius, geometry, and spirit to make you smile.

Adapted from the catalog article for the international exhibition "Poetry in Paper," Krapina City Gallery, Croatia, 2008.

CONTENTS

ACKNOWLEDGMENTS

Though it's grown enormously in recent years, the origami community is still very close knit. It is a pleasure to have so many people to thank directly for their help. Let me start, though, with the wider world. I'd like to express my special gratitude to the Witztum family, Allan and Ann especially, for nourishment in various forms these past years and reliable high conversation on origami, botany, embryology, pollen grains that fold up, books, art, museums, and everything else. I'm grateful also to Bradley Ruffle, for the friendship and the professional art photography.

Origami has quite a few consummate artists in it, yet it is still an under-appreciated field, which makes those of us working in it comrades-in-arms of sorts. Even so I am surprised by the generous and extensive help offered, sometimes on the slenderest of acquaintanceships. For specific and essential assistance on this book I wish to thank:

Jose Ignacio Royo Pietro—for discussions of curve-folding geometry and detailed reactions to drafts; and both Ignacio and Herman Mariano for testing the animal diagrams.

Robert J. Lang, for a highly interesting discussion in early 2009 of David Huffman's work, which unleashed a cascade of creativity that's affected this book.

Herman van Goubergen, for exchanges on one of our shared interests, concentric folds, and characteristically sharp and quick insights.

And then there is the inspiration, friendship and hopes of unnamed individuals in far-flung countries such as Central America, Spain, Vietnam, Central Europe, and all the other places where origami is now finding a handhold. I am grateful to colleagues and role-models, to gifted students who focus one's thoughts, even to competitors who've kept me on my toes. You know who you are.

I would be remiss if I did not at least mention Roman Diaz in Uruguay, Giang Dinh of Vietnam (and now U.S.A.), and Polly Verity of Scotland for their field-defining work in animal design, expressive figuration, and curve-folding respectively. With you and the maybe five or six others now pushing the limits, this field is set to explode.

Greetings, all!

Saadya
Beersheva, Israel, 2010

SCULPTURAL ORIGAMI

All good origami is fun; some good origami is also sculpture. I don't think anyone can dispute the high artistic aims of the father of modern origami, Akira Yoshizawa (1911–2005). When the origami historian David Lister, visiting a Yoshizawa exhibition in Kyoto, enthuses about the "gorillas with impressively fierce facial features," the "group of hippopotamuses which successfully caught the enormous bulk of the animals," the "lively, arguing parrots engaged in a squawking quarrel"—it is very clear that the paper-folding in question is not some technical pastime, but an expressive art that draws on full capacities of study, empathy, light-heartedness, obstinacy, innovation, and transmissibility, the very traits historically demanded of sculptors at the highest levels. It is quite right that museums have been paying attention to this founding figure, and are regarding his works as sculptures in the full sense of the word.

Within the field today, however, there is a certain tug of war over what the artistic elements of origami actually are. On one hand, the individual's touch on the sheet of paper is essential: only the inventor of that specific paper-fold can breath life into it in his or her particular way. On the other hand, a criterion of a good origami model is its replicability, by others as well as the creator. To the extent that origami is a social art—meant to bring joy to others by enabling them to reproduce the form—the element of the idiosyncratic can be seen as negative. Folders around the world rightly demand clear procedures they can follow, enjoy, and appreciate the logic of. They expect results that can be measured against a photograph of the model, letting them check off a box with satisfaction: "I've done X's Panda." (And there it is sitting on the bookshelf.) At the extreme, if this concept predominates, the artist's touch on the

model will entirely disappear, though a touch of sorts will remain on the design-logic, the geometry, and the elegance of its fold sequence.

So some good origami may be sculpture, but the art that is within origami isn't *only* that of sculpture. In titling this book *Sculptural Origami*, I am not suggesting that this is some superior form of paper-folding; only that it is one in which the expressive elements have been given freer reign.

My ideas on this subject have evolved: this book reflects that evolution. A quarter century ago I began my career in origami as a designer of animals. I like to play with the finished creatures—move the legs this way and that, adjust the posture, toy with the facial expression. So I designed for people like me, taking pains, for instance, that the limbs of the finished model not be locked into one position. It is sometimes thought that designing for flexibility is easier than designing for consistency of result, since the former presents a softer target to aim for. That's not necessarily the case: the fold sequence must still begin from an uncut square, and still ideally be strictly referenced, logical, efficient in paper usage and in number of steps, geometric, pleasant to fold, vastly simpler than the competition's, and if followed correctly yield a pleasing final form, preferably in three dimensions. Only now that form must also allow *variation*. It isn't always easy to pull off.

This is a path that's been trod by others. Several of the top modern designers, like Bernie Peyton, Giang Dinh, and Roman Diaz pursue a similar ideal in some of their work, often to great effect. In this approach to expression and interpretation something inherent to origami is being highlighted—its open-endedness and playfulness—while a further inherent aspect of origami—its sociality and communicability, is being preserved. For the end-folder, too, is invited into the form-making process—is being encouraged to put his or her stamp on the final model.

As said, design for expressiveness isn't easy. I left origami for almost a dozen years, in part because of what struck me as its limitations on artistry and expression. When I came back to the field, I took up the problem of making *faces,* resuming in paper plus foil studies I'd begun in 1987 in foil alone. The faces I was after were to be sculptural and realistic, not so-called "masks," which had been done.

Yet this time I took a different approach to the problem of expression. I decided to stop worrying about communicability or replicability altogether. The works were to be completely idiosyncratic or individual, just as in the other arts.

So I tried to forget everything that I knew about paper-folding. As I viewed things at the time: here was the sheet of foil paper, about a foot wide by two or three feet long, sitting on the desk. I would dig fingers into it and wrestle out a form much as one sticks one's hands into a lump of clay: a blind tactile digging. There would be no rules except what the paper itself imposed. And what the fingers found, I would leave, without a thought to whether someone else could do it too.

Of course, it is not quite the same as the lump of clay; you still need *something* to grasp and manipulate. But, as it turns out, you don't need a whole lot—a pleat here and there, some three-dimensionality formed by a triangular crimp. Soon a different aspect of origami, its *austerity,* the doing a lot with a little, came to be a guiding principle for me, possibly as expiation for all I was throwing out (not just repeatability and sociality but also the square and its geometry). I decided there would be as few lines as possible, with much of the work left to the dreaded "shaping." There would be no folding on a flat surface: everything would be done in the air. No colors, at least none of the bright happy-colored "kami" papers that makes so much origami seem childlike. It would now be all plain brown paper—if expression was to be through form, let it be form *unadorned.* No use of the corners of the sheet, and so, no proper "flaps." Surface, not edge or corner, is what would be manipulated henceforth.

This ascetic, almost origami hostile mood passed, I am glad to say, but many of the faces in this book were made while under its sway. For blind tactility is all very well, but eventually you get curious about what you're doing, and the paper is obeying certain rules no matter how hard you try to break them. Maybe by trying to break them you find out what they are. The various problems of working in three dimensions, and the more focused problem of making three-dimensional faces with as few non-natural lines as possible, have optimal solutions which I or anyone else working on them will gravitate toward. That's because the material for making a feature has to come from somewhere, the folds that result have to be hidden away somehow, and there are worse, better, and best ways of doing this. In short, systematic questions arise, and keep reappearing; the surface freedom and expressive variation rides on top of a logic which is—dare I say it—communicable.

Tackling the problems of faces meant thinking a good deal about manipulating sheets long after they have ceased to be flat. This effort also pulled me deeper into the subject of folding *curves.* For non-flat surfaces are as likely to be curving as planar, and any folds made subsequently in the curving surfaces will themselves, for geometric reasons, necessarily be curve folds.

Now, one of the properties of a curve fold may be called its intrinsic "variability" or "unspecificity." In essence, whenever one curved crease allows a surface to partially fold up and compact itself, there is always a family of related curves that will *also* do the trick in roughly the same way. Moreover, there is no "origami" way to specify which curve from within the family to choose: you can't align one flap to another to locate a particular curve fold, as you would do in "normal" origami to locate a particular straight fold, because of another law that says that walls to either side of a curved crease can't be brought flush to each other. To specify a particular curved crease exactly, you need to introduce tools from outside origami, like a compass or a plotter.

It follows that curve folds are *inherently* unreferenced and less "communicable;" if done by eye and by hand they are likely to be done differently by each eye and each hand. I say this with special reference to those who complain about the use of so-called "judgment folds" in origami: if you are making curve folds, and are not using outside tools, "judgment" can't be avoided. (Horrors!) Expression is, so to speak, built into a curve fold.

But even if the curves themselves are intrinsically unreferenced and idiosyncratic, the principles which govern them are not: they are public and universal. Some of those laws can be applied and turned into origami discoveries, like the circular models that I close this book with. These are purely geometric models, easy to reproduce with homemade equipment, and, however three-dimensional and "sculptural" they may be, they allow no expression whatsoever. Even so, they are worth communicating. It seems that sociality, for all the effort to flee it, returns; and with it the built-in origami instinct to teach, and to touch.

President Shimon Peres, his mentor Ben-Gurion, and the author.
(Photo taken at the Henkin Gallery, Holon, Israel, January 2005.)

PART I

FACES

Each of the faces and heads in this book started life as a rectangle of paper glued to stiff aluminum foil, which was then bent and manipulated into its final shape, without cutting. The stiffness of the aluminum lets the final form hold its shape well on its own; depending on the project, further stabilizers may be added. The curvaceous three-dimensional form of the sculptures sometimes surprises people given that the skin of the medium is paper. This shapeliness does not result from pressing the sheet into a mold or wetting and somehow stretching it, but results entirely from folding processes, some of which involve curve folding. These processes, when used with the right materials, permit the representation of a wide range of physiognomies, with all the exquisite sensitivity that a paper surface affords. More than just a form of origami, which it certainly is, I think of this as a new sculptural medium, competing for a place beside the ancient traditional media of stone, clay, wood, and metal.

The paper joined to the foil is usually the plain brown paper known as "kraft" or "postal wrap." When flat, this material is about as poor and dull as it can be. Add a few delicate curved creases though, and it jumps to life, gaining a tenderness or vulnerability that is easily as evocative as skin. Curve-creased brown paper looks a bit like clay; with whiter paper and scored curves, it looks like plaster; with a slight crumple, it acquires the texture of stone. There is no need to add color—the play of shadows across the surface is arresting enough.

For human representation, the humbleness of this material is, I think, key. The cheeky engagement of this negligible bit of flimsiness with the viewer; naturally prompts questions about the source of the impressiveness of any living face. For flesh really is just dust and ashes, without the animating principle. Here the ashy integument is brown paper, and the animating principle is origami. The effect is the exact opposite of that of stone sculpture, which aims at a defiance of time. Here, as in all origami, with this material that breathes, there is a suggestion of transience and mutability that is "just like life."

The emergence of three-dimensionality from flatness is perhaps the oldest of themes in sculpture, dating back thirty or forty thousand years from the time that a crude chisel was first taken to a stone wall, and what would have been a painting became a bas-relief. Somehow origami, the newest of the sculptural arts despite its centuries-old roots, is able to recapture some of that old wonder. As other designers of human forms in paper-folds will confirm, the faces that emerge between ones hands seem to come from another time and place, a blend of images from Egyptian antiquity, Mesopotamia, early Greece, Buddhist art, the Classic or Medieval period, or other halls in a museum-saturated subconscious. Without thinking much: letting the intellect busy itself with solving the technical problems that folding presents at every turn, while keeping an eye out for what counts as sculpture—the figures emerge. Strangely, this art seems to be absolved of the need to make a contemporary statement, to reflect this or that current cultural crisis or trend. Instead it is allowed to reflect nothing but the perennial requirements of simplicity, intelligence, spirit, and empathy. Apparently, with origami taking its rightful place alongside the traditional arts, the whole history of the sculptural tradition is being set loose to recapitulate itself—and that emergence is enough.

Longevity, Stabilization and Preservation

Paper was invented over two thousand years ago; paper objects have been preserved for almost as long. Drawings, and later, books printed on quality paper have lasted many centuries in essentially pristine condition. Therefore the supposed perishability of paper is an illusion, or an artifact of the poor-quality papers that came into fashion a century ago. Even those newer acid-heavy papers, when glued to a substrate and sealed with a varnish, can be expected to endure.

Folded paper's vulnerability to change is real enough; what is made with a fold can be unmade with an unfold. But here too, methods have been developed to preserve an origami object in its final form. For works in pure paper, Akira Yoshizawa developed the method of "wet-folding," in which a thick paper (made with some sizing added) is wetted slightly before and during folding. This allows even stiff papers to crease without cracking, gives rise to a "meatier" look in the folds, allows curved surfaces to retain their shape, and then, as the model dries, lets it harden into its final form. At the Tikotin Museum of Japanese Art, I was privileged to handle some of Yoshizawa's wet-folded works dating from the 1930s; they are as stiff and unyielding today as they presumably were when they were first set to dry.

Origami has changed. Modern technical folding, with its highly-detailed models, requires a much larger number of folds and fold layers. Thick paper can't be used for this purpose, as it would bulk up unmanageably. So modern origami uses thin paper, and the stabilizer of choice today for thin-paper origami is *methyl cellulose*, applied before or during folding. Methyl cellulose has the rare property of stiffening the model without altering the dry papery appearance of the surface.

I sometimes use methyl cellulose for my animal origami, but almost never for the faces. There, though

I've reverted to a "thick paper/thin folding" approach which (probably in that respect alone) is similar to Yoshizawa's, the material is usually not pure paper but paper glued to one or both sides of a stiff aluminum foil. Foil paper isn't really helped by moisture or methyl cellulose; the shape is held by the folds in metal, and this metal is inert. Here, a different solution is called for. The *surface* may be protected, not from denting but from staining, by a thin wash of water-based acrylic matte varnish. If the *form* needs stabilizing, this can be done by applying varnishes and fills to the insides, thinly or thickly as required. Most of the stronger stabilizers, like liquid polyurethane, stain paper and vastly change its appearance, so a layer of water-based acrylic must be applied to the inside first. (Folded aluminum foil has tiny holes that will let any damaging liquids through to the surface if not sealed beforehand.) Large hollows can be filled by urethane foam, but this too must be done in layers as foam tends to swell uncontrollably and will press out a weak paper wall. Heavier fills such as plaster can be used if desired, once the surface has been adequately stiffened.

All the above applies to sculptures with a paper skin; but one can also choose to use fabric for the surface, and the folding technique also works well with pure metals like copper foil, thin lead sheeting, and assorted steel meshes. At larger scales, chicken wire can be folded via these techniques and used as a substrate for plaster or cement coatings. Paper works may also be bronze-cast using the lost wax method. And nowadays you can scan a surface with a three-dimensional scanner and have a machine carve out a large-scale facsimile—even from stone. In short, all the tricks and techniques of the practicing figure artist, of both the old and newer sorts, are applicable to "sculptural origami."

Cone Flattening Technique

To begin our study of faces, let's look at how cones are made and how cones can be flattened.

A cone in paper is formed by putting a triangular crimp with its apex in the interior of the sheet (fig. A).

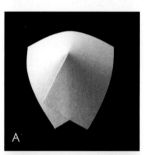

You'll notice right away that while the cone's surface curves around the apex, you can easily turn that surface into a series of planes, by adding a few open-mountain folds from the apex to the edges to form a pyramid (fig. B). If you do so, you haven't "flattened" the cone from its three-dimensional shape to a two-dimensional one, but you have "flattened" it in the sense of getting rid of all its curvature. Full flattening can be achieved by squeezing the form through the apex and/or adding suitable valley folds—always with the folds reaching all the way to the sheet's cut edge (fig. C).

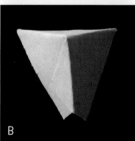

A cone left rounded can also be partially flattened, or at least reduced in height, by sinking it one or more times through concentric circles centered around the apex (fig. D), or by suitable nested ellipses. If you do that, however, by definition, none of the creases will be straight, and one of the most basic laws of curve-folding geometry is that once there is a curved crease anywhere in a sheet, the form can never be fully flattened. So height reduction and a "flat on average" shape is the best that is attainable by this curving back-and-forth method.

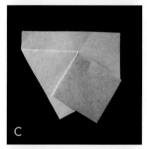

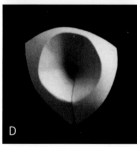

There is also a procedure that combines the best and the worst features of the above. Starting with the cone, you can pinch a piece of the apex along a straight line—a line that *doesn't* reach to the edge of the sheet—folding that line over as a mountain fold (fig. E), or sinking the pinched off material through the line (fig. F). The cone's height will be lowered by the amount pinched off, but the surface will not have been made flat, as it was in the pyramid. Nevertheless *some* surface curvature will have been eliminated, and the region near the line will be flatter. So we will have made partial progress toward the twin goals of lowering height and reducing curvature.

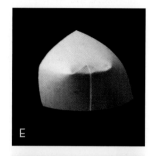

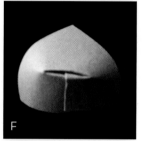

Notice that the edges of the pinched line also interact with the surface of the former cone by creating apexes of new cones; there are now two apexes instead of one. These new apexes can also be pinched off (fig. G), and those pinched off as well, ad infinitum; the more this is done, the less surface curvature will there be. Here too, as long as the pinches do not extend to the edges of the sheet, there will always be some height and some curvature remaining. On the plus side, since the pinched folds are all straight and flat, this pinched material can be manipulated in standard origami ways, without having to deal with curve-folding issues.

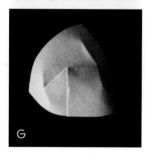

The upshot of all of this is that you can manipulate the cone-flattening process so that as a cone gives up height, the surface, as viewed from above, gains in texture. Some of that texture can involve curved creases and some can involve straight ones; it is up to you. Some of the texture can be kept in its three-dimensional state (the noses in my sculptures), while some of it can be flattened to form visual lines (overly conical cheeks get flattened naturalistically with short lines sunk at the sides of the nose). So with cone flattening, as you trade in three-dimensionality for two, you can "draw" and "sculpt."

Remember that what you draw does not have to extend all the way across the surface, and what you sculpt can protrude largely without benefit of hard folds. You still need at least *one* crimp line that extends all the way to one edge, to form the cone. The net effect of this absence of line can be dramatic; features can seem to emerge from the paper inexplicably, as if the surface had suddenly been allowed locally to stretch (the "Nine-Faced Jar" and

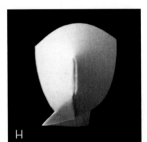

"Blockhead Confucius" are good examples).

Thus far I've been describing how to "subtract" curvature from a cone, but you can also add curvature to it, and not necessarily at the cone's original apex. Without adding a new line visually, you can add a second, shorter crimp to the one that first formed the cone (fig. H); you will then have a surface with two apexes and greater curvature. I use this concept sometimes to add three-

dimensionality where it is needed. While the nose is the most protuberant part of the face and is usually the tip of the "main" cone, the mouth, too, needs to stand out. One way to do that is to add a second apex below the nose, then sink it (fig. I).

In terms of surface geometry, a two-apexed "cone" made subtractively (by pinching the apex of an acute cone) is no different from a two-apexed "cone" made additively (by adding a second crimp to a shallow cone). For many origami reasons the subtractive approach is cleaner and preferable. One disadvantage, though, is that subtraction always leaves you with shallower apexes than the one you started with, and the shallower the apex, the less you can do with it. The additive approach, by contrast, lets you "tank up" conic curvature at any new apex, making the new cone tip as acute as you like.

In what I've described so far, the cone-forming crimps have all been single crimps. Single crimps are by definition asymmetric, and for design purposes it is often advisable to stay symmetric by using a double crimp that meets at a center line. But one advantage of single crimps is that you can add many new apex points along the same line, alternating the direction of the crimp, each time locking in the segment above it. Such additive interlacing can be

done indefinitely—or at least until you run out of paper.

The various ideas above all dealt with cones made from a single thickness of paper, but they work equally well when the thickness is greater—e.g. two sheets or two layers of the same sheet. Where there are multiple layers, there is also a means of locking in the three-dimensionality: slip the excess material from the triangular crimp between the layers (fig. J). Now the crimp is no longer free to come undone. With foil-backed paper this is less of an issue, but for pure-paper-folding this is a very nice solution for locking paper into a three-dimensional shape. Unless I'm mistaken, a similar "layered-cone lock" is used by the designers Joseph Wu and Roman Diaz, among others, and is one of the set of maneuvers once given the ungainly name of "dry-tension-folding."

Man of Affairs *(2004)*, *17 inches. From an uncut rectangle of paper-foil-paper.*

The Spinster *(2004), 17 inches. From an uncut rectangle of foil-backed paper.*

I was and remain impressed by the great Israeli sculptress Chana Orloff, and can only struggle to achieve in a paper fold some semblance of what she manages in her wood sculptures.

Siddhartha *(2004)*, *18 inches. From an uncut rectangle of foil-backed paper.*

Leonardo da Vinci *(2004), 17 inches. From an uncut rectangle of foil-backed paper.*

This work began as a test of a folding concept, not an attempt to depict anyone in particular. But at some point the resemblance to the famous self-portrait became apparent, so I pulled my art book off the shelf and completed my sculpture of Leonardo. Later I discovered Melzi's sketch (the only known portrait of Leonardo from another angle), and was pleased to see that my three-dimensional interpretation was not entirely off.

Buddhist Priest *(2004)*, *32 inches. From an uncut rectangle of foil-backed paper.*

*During a "Buddhist" art phase, I was trying to see how much form could be generated
in a sheet from just two or three hard folds (an exercise in minimalism). In this sculpture
I aimed for certain amount of presence, but also for the simplicity, worldliness, and
humor that I associate with Buddhism.*

David Ben-Gurion *(2008)*, *16 inches. From an uncut rectangle of paper-foil-paper.*

David Ben-Gurion was Israel's first prime minister, a hard-headed, far-sighted leader, sorely missed in these times. His signature hairdo, at least, turns out to be readily reproducible in origami: as crumples that bend out from the sides of a bald head. Two versions of "Ben-Gurion" were made. The first now belongs to the collector Dietrich Mateschitz, of Salzburg; the second to Zemach Sternberg, of New York.

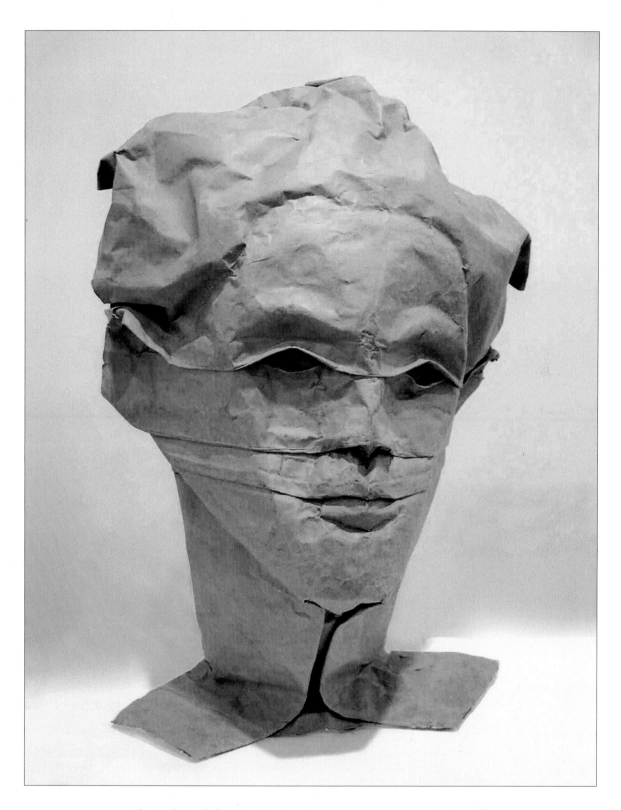

Classical Head *(2004)*, *24 inches. From an uncut rectangle. Urethane fill.*

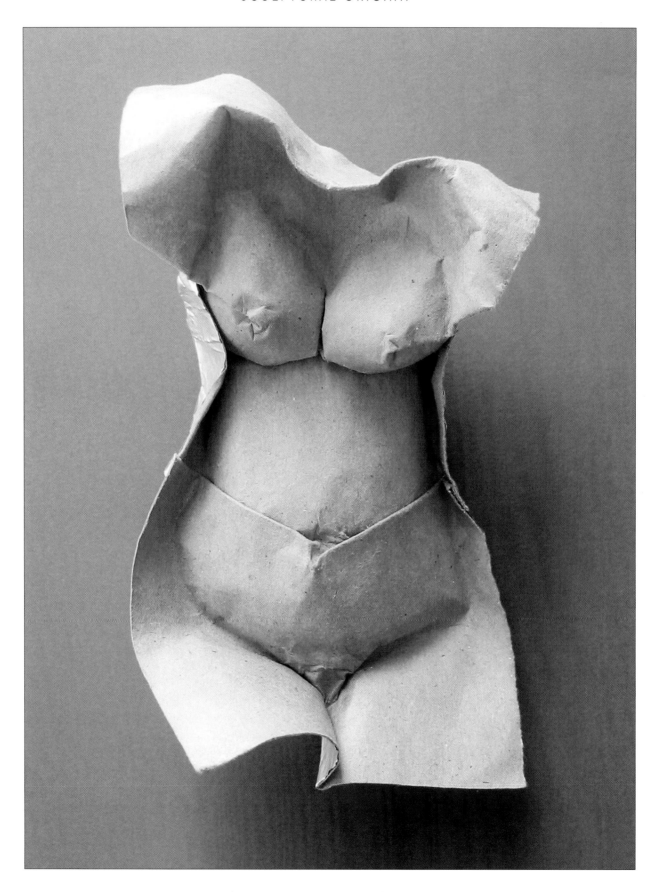

Torso (2004), 8 inches. From an uncut rectangle of foil-backed paper.

Ernestine *(2005)*, *18 inches. From an uncut rectangle of paper-foil-paper.*

Flat Face *(2009), 8 inches. From an uncut rectangle of foil-backed paper.*

*The emergence of three-dimensionality from flatness, and the play between the two,
is a constant source of interest.*

Jar of Muses *(2006), 14 inches wide. From an uncut rectangle of foil-backed paper.*

How can the more free form, curvaceous sort of origami fit within conventional origami and its rigid planar geometry? This is one stab at an answer. The basic shape is a cylinder: a rectangle the far edges of which are glued together. The lower part of the cylinder tapers via crimp-folds, and its base is twist-folded shut.

Kiss Me *(2004)*, *12 inches. From an uncut rectangle of paper-foil-paper.*

Eastern Royal Figurine *(2005)*, *8 inches. From an uncut rectangle of foil-backed paper.*

Bearded Head *(2010), 10 inches. From an uncut square of foil-backed paper.*

The Debutante *(2007)*, *16 inches. From an uncut rectangle of paper-foil-paper.*

OPPOSITE: Buddha *(2008)*, *8 inches. From an uncut square of foil-backed paper.*

ABOVE: Japanese Businessman *(2007)*, *6 inches. Wet-folded from one rectangle of thick paper.*

I don't know where one gathers visual ideas about people from distant cultures.
In the case of my Japan it is usually a mixture of images from diverse periods, picked up
from museums, books, and movies—especially from the films of Akira Kurosawa.

OPPOSITE: Peasant Head *(2007), 9 inches. From an uncut rectangle of foil-backed paper.*

ABOVE: Molly, v. IV *(2008), 10 inches. From an uncut rectangle of foil-backed paper.*

This curly-headed young woman is not some particular living individual, but now that I have folded four such "Mollies," it is starting to feel like she is.

Conventional origami three-dimensional methods tend to generate faces that are masculine and "experienced," possibly because of the lines that cut across the face or the jutting features. So it's been a particular challenge, working through many of the figures in this book, to produce a fresh-cheeked female in her full bloom of innocence.

Madame Tsen-Li *(2006), 7 inches. From an uncut rectangle of paper-foil-paper.*

ABOVE: Nine-Faced Jar *(2009)*, *12 inches. From an uncut rectangle of foil-backed paper.*

The "Jar of Muses" concept needed revisiting; and I'd been affected by the recent sight of portals to churches in Spain, with their myriad medieval faces. As always there is a technical idea to be explored along with the artistic one. Here it is the "cone flattening" technique, in which textured and protuberant contours seems to emerge from a smooth and flat state without the benefit of hard folds or hidden material. So that the surface seems to be doing one thing that paper can't: stretch.

RIGHT: The Nine Faces (Detail): *Faces on the jar.*

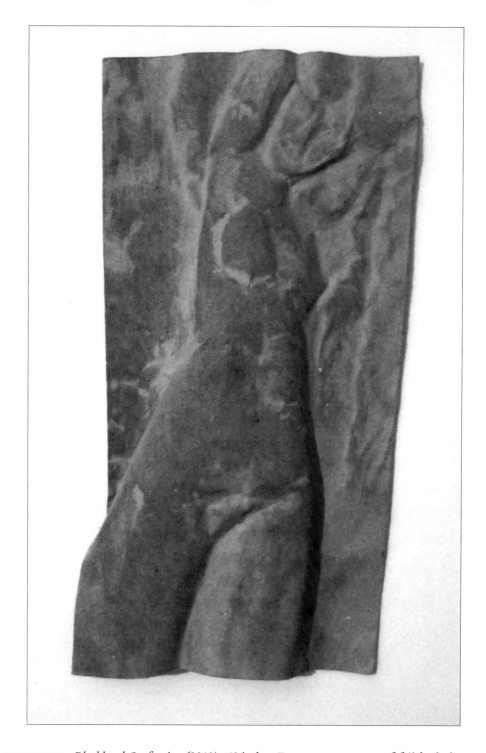

OPPOSITE: *Blockhead Confuscius (2010), 12 inches. From an uncut square of foil-backed paper.*

I had just read Chinese author Ma Jian's Red Dust, *and was struck by his fine head in the thumbnail photograph. For this face, I was also thinking of the quite different head of the origami artist Joseph Wu, and of traditional representations of Confucius, and possibly also of the beards on Egyptian sarcophagi.*

There were two technical problems to be solved: an old one, how to make a face from folds without introducing non-naturalistic creases; and a newer one, how to make features erupt suddenly from a smooth and flat expanse of paper, seemingly in violation of paper's non-elasticity. This is the result.

ABOVE: *Stepping Out (2004), 7 inches. From an uncut rectangle of foil-backed paper, gouache-rub, post-fold.*

PART II

ANIMALS

Animals folded from squares constitute the core of traditional, pure origami, that is, origami made from single square sheets of paper, without cutting or gluing. (Geometric forms made out of single or multiple sheets constitute the next largest branch of the field.) Pure origami can of course be used to make inanimate objects as well—a jackknife, a racing car, a sailboat—but animals still form the bulk of this field, and in a way also its heart. There is something particularly appealing about getting a recognizable animal at the end of a fold sequence; with the final creature often strangely lifelike—touched somehow with the charm and innocence of real animals. Origami is related not just to the lifelike, but to life itself (all animals, as embryos, take shape through the folding processes of *gastrulation* and *neurulation*) as well as to the study of living forms. I would venture to say that despite the relative youth of paper-folding, more species of animals have already been modeled in this medium than in the entire history of human sculpture in all other media *combined*. It seems that origami is offering a new way to sculpturally reconsider the full range of the world's faunal taxonomy.

When a grandmother brings her grandchildren to the origami exhibit at the museum and says, "look at the rabbit," "look at the horsey," that may seem to cheapen the products as art. Actually it is more surprising that there should be this commonality of reaction in the first place. Why *are* paper-folded animals more effective in exciting this "recognition impulse" than sculpted ivory figurines? What makes them more "lifelike," lets them engage our affections so readily? I have no good answer to these questions.

For adults, if there's a guilty pleasure here (guilty for being no different than a five-year-old's), it is tempered by an awareness of the intellectual effort invested in pulling this shape from a square. Simultaneous with recognizing the animal for what it is, is a recognition of the *jeu d'esprit* bound up in its creation. Like the punch-line of a joke, the folded object is where it all comes together. There is something relieving and light, innocent and intelligent and self-contained to a paper-folded creature—qualities we recognize, it may be, in the animals themselves.

ABOVE: Camel *(2006/2010)*, *7 inches. From an uncut square of shaggy-fiber paper.*

OPPOSITE: Wader *(2009)*, *9 inches. Dry folded from an uncut square.*

From a variant of a bird base.

Heron *(1990/2005)*, *5 inches. From an uncut square.*

A development of the bird-frog base.

Pelican *(2009), 6 inches. Wet folded from an uncut square.*

Dove *(ca. 2009)*, *11 inches. From an uncut square.*

Made out of a puffed out bird base. A distant relation to the Yoshizawa Pigeon.

Flitting Birds *(1987/2006), 5 inches. From an uncut square.*

The "cut-edge" of the paper square, held out in the wings, seem to flitter with a bird's nervous motion.
Except for their puffy heads, a recent improvement, this was one of my very first ideas as a designer in 1987.
It is a straightforward development of the logic of the stretched, blintzed bird base.

Bird with Shadow *(2007), 5 inches. Dry folded from an uncut square.*

Sparrows *(2007),* *7 inches. From uncut squares of gift wrap and tissue paper.*

OPPOSITE: Chameleon *(designed 1993, folded 2004), 6 inches. From an uncut square of lizard paper.*

The Chameleon diagrams can be found on page 85.

ABOVE: Carton Horse *(1993/2009), 14 inches. Wet folded from an uncut square of carton paper.*

Akira Yoshizawa pioneered the technique of adding moisture to stiff papers while folding to make them more pliable, prevent cracking, and allow the model to harden while drying into its curved form. The idea of applying the technique specifically to carton paper was developed by Spanish folder Carlos Hermoso Ríos, who taught it to me.

OPPOSITE: Three Poses for a Horse *(1993/2006)*, *5 to 6 inches. From an uncut square.*

Diagrams for two of the poses can be found on page 89.

ABOVE: Horses and Riders *(1991)*, *6 to 7 inches. Each figure is from an uncut square of contact paper and kitchen foil.*

OPPOSITE: Monkey *(designed 1991, folded 2010), 8 inches. From an uncut square.*

A variation of the idea used for the Chameleon.

ABOVE: Vase of Gladioli *(2005), 5 inches. From an uncut square.*

Yes—flora, not fauna. It is made from a base related to that of the Cat.

Modern technical origami generates a large number of "points" (tips of flaps) in its models, but this often builds up an unsightly bulk of pleats concealable only if very thin paper is used. Here, rather than hide it, I made it into foliage.

Cats *(1990), 6 and 10 inches. From uncut squares of kitchen foil and flock-cloth contact paper.*

The Cat diagrams can be found on page 81.

Camels in Beersheva *(2006)*, *6 inches. From uncut squares of kraft paper.*

Lion *(2005), 5 inches. From an uncut square.*

From the same animal base as the Horse.

Standing Figures *(1989/2009)*, *7 and 4 inches. From uncut paper squares.*

The Standing Man diagrams can be found on page 78.

PART III
CURVES

Curving surfaces and lines can create mystery and grace in any sculptural medium—the concavities and convexities generating dramatic, graduated shadows; the snaking lines suggesting fluidity, indefiniteness, movement. But folded curves in paper are something else again. Paper's natural flatness, its most intuitively basic characteristic, is contradicted. The viewer half knows that this is paper, and is charmed; and half gropes for recognition in other familiar media, like plaster or stone. If it *is* paper, surely it must have been wetted and stretched, or alternatively squeezed into a mold and compressed; how else could that visible surface have become so rounded, so protuberant, seemingly malleable as clay? Yet none of this has happened. Paper is not plastic, and here it has been left in its native state, unstretched and unsqueezed. So to the arresting visual qualities that all sculpted curves can have, curves in paper add an element of *magic*.

Within the origami world, one hears also that curve folding is more "mathematically complex" or specially "computational" than folding of the usual sort, or that it's otherwise more difficult. This seems a bit overdone to me. Curve folds really *are* different; the laws of curve folding preclude some of the most basic operations of straight-line origami, (like "align one folded edge to another"). Sculptures with folded curves can also arouse more *complex emotions* than origami of the usual planar sort; and, as said, the shapes can be confounding to an eye not used to them. They are not, for all that, necessarily more difficult—not even mathematically. At the risk of revealing a few trade secrets: paper has no objection whatsoever to being rolled into a cylinder, or flexed into a cone, or left flat,

or all three (smoothly if the transitions are right), and paper can be folded along a curved crease quite easily provided the surfaces to either side are also allowed to curve. This means that good deal of surface curvature can be achieved by some *very primitive operations*. Combine two or three of these moves though, along with a few extra tricks, and soon your audience won't recognize the result as behaving in any way like paper "should." Magic!

My work in curve folds divides into two broad sorts. First are the curving tessellations: patterns of curves that systematically repeat. I had been seeking a solution to the problem of *hair* for my figures, some bit of texture that would also allow a sheet to bend in two directions at once, as the dome of the top of the head requires, and these curly patterns do the job nicely. Then the topic began to interest me independently. What lets a pattern of curve-folds tessellate? What lets it stay "flat-on-average?" How compressible is each pattern, and why? What happens to the aspect-ratio under compression? What lets the average surface stay flat, or have a positive or a negative curvature? Can curve-fold patterns interact with straight-fold ones? While these are all "geometric" questions, they are driven throughout by the aim of making something pretty, something that can be used expressively.

The second category is concentric folds. This field, I am pleased to say, was invented by a proper artist, Joseph Albers, of Bauhaus fame, who in his design workshops in the 1920s or 30s assigned the exercise of folding up disks of paper scored with concentric circles. This exercise was part of his pioneering work in a field that today we would call "collapsible origami."

The Squeeze Hairdo. Curving tessellations allow a sheet to flex in two directions at once.

Now, these disks, as they fold, don't stay flat on average as one might expect. Instead they twist and buckle, forming a saddle-like shape said by mathematicians to have "negative curvature." The reason for this is that the circles are being pulled toward the center by the folds, so their radiuses are getting shorter, but meanwhile their circumferences have stayed the same length, despite the law that says $C = 2\pi R$. So the circles accommodate this by breaking from the plane, rising and falling in a wave to eat up their excess length.

This same "twisty-surface" phenomenon was explored extensively by the magician and artist Thoki Yenn, who used an annulus with concentric circles rather than a solid disk as the starting form—an annulus being more flexible for twisting purposes.

Yet I wanted to *avoid* all this Albers-Yenn twisting. For me, "subduing" curve-folds involves bringing them back to the basic language of origami, i.e. flatness (even if only average flatness) and straight folds. With concentric circles, an average flatness can be recovered by introducing a single cut on the radius, which allows the excess circumference to be taken up by overlap, and any twisting to be avoided. Hence my "Concentric Winder": the circles wind up on top of each other indefinitely, as the circles grow smaller. But concentric curves can also be brought under control by suitable folds, without any cutting at all. This is what I do with my "Sphere-from-a-Circle": with a few simple folds a disk can fold up directly into a ball. What a surprise! The latter form, which by rights Albers should have discovered eighty years ago, is my most "geometric" model to date: still "sculptural," even if not at all expressive. With it I close.

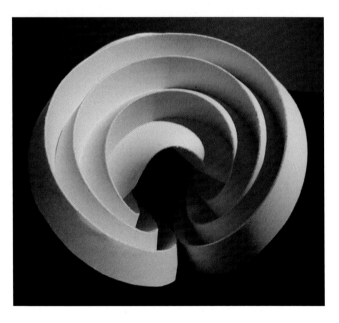

The Albers-Yenn Effect. A disk scored with concentric circles is forced into an eerie buckling.

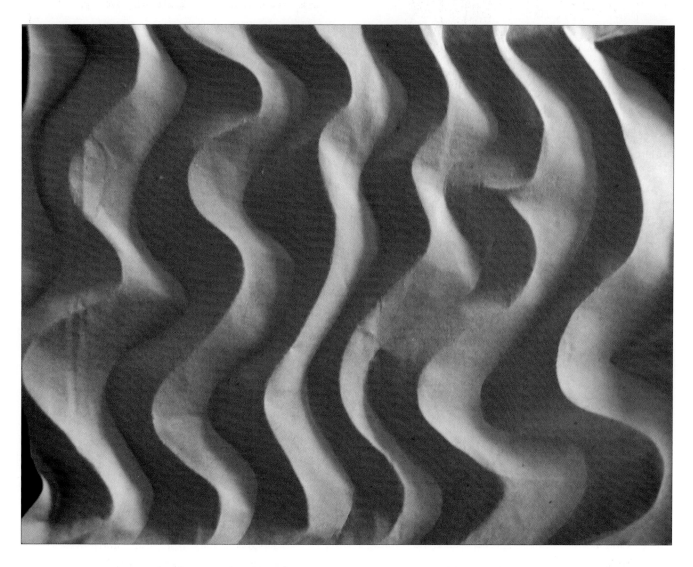

Sand Waves *(2005)*, *16 inches. From an uncut rectangle of foil-backed paper.*

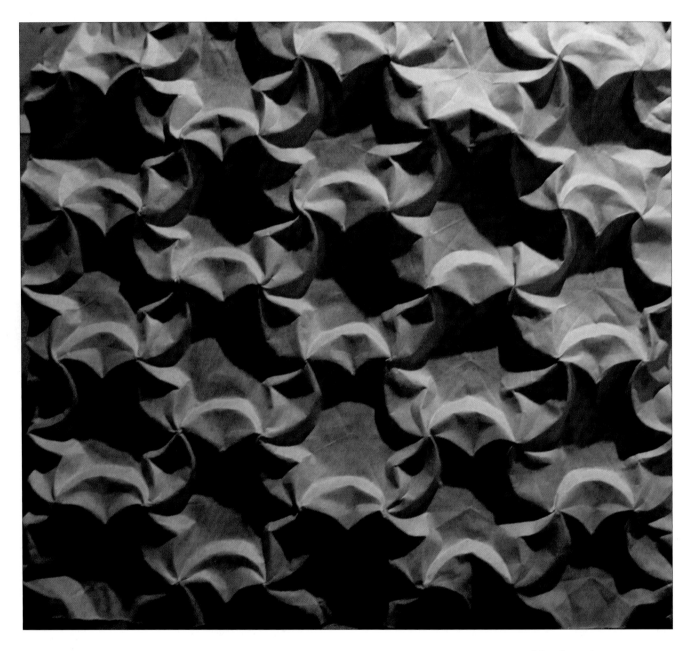

ABOVE: Curving Tesselation, Hexagon Grid *(2005), 24 inches. From an uncut rectangle of foil-backed paper.*

OPPOSITE: Spiral Curving Tessellation, Triangle Grid *(2005), 16 inches.*
From an uncut rectangle of foil-backed paper.

The Spiral Curving Tessellation diagrams can be found on page 97.

Clam-Shell Pattern *(2006), 12 inches. From an uncut surface of foil-backed paper.*

Ripple-Edge Flower *(2008)*, *6 inches. From an uncut rectangle of chromatography paper with glued edges.*

Peacock Fan *(2008)*, *14 inches. From an uncut rectangle of chromatography paper.*

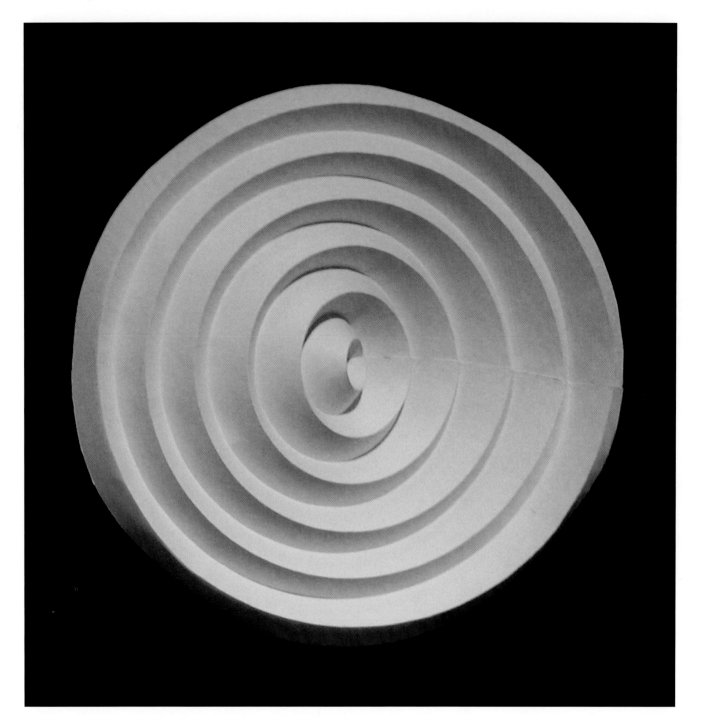

Huffmanesque *(2009), 14 inches. From an uncut paper semicircle with glued edges.*

David Huffman's haunting Concentric Circles from the 1970s (paralleling similar work done then by Ron Resch), known through a single photograph, has long been a mystery to many. This is my reconstruction of its idea, with a few circles added as a proof-of-concept. Essentially, a pattern of evenly-spaced concentric circles has its mountain-folds and its valley-folds dissociated and slightly offset. A wide wedge is cut out and cut edges are joined as if to make a cone. While geometry states that one or both sets of curves must be ellipses, true circles work reasonably well—and can be plotted with simpler equipment.

Curve-Fold Fountain *(2009), 6 inches. From a circle of paper, radius cut.*

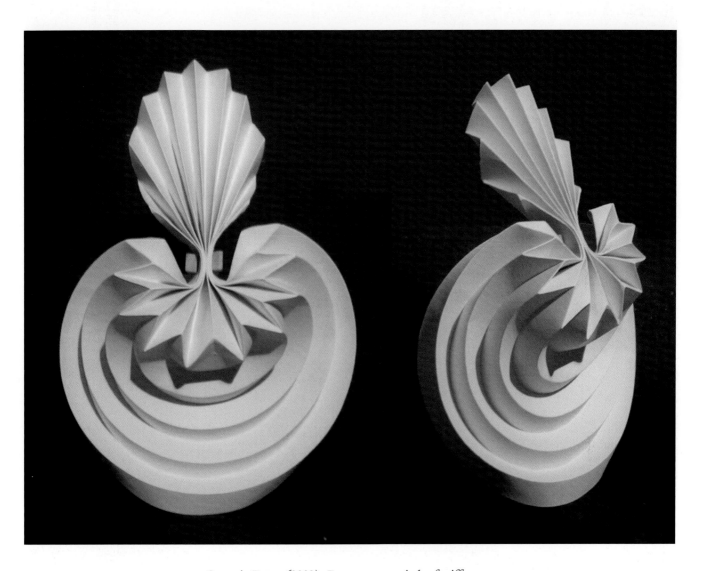

Organic Form *(2009). From an uncut circle of stiff paper.*

Parallel straight-line corrugations can collapse flat; parallel curving corrugations cannot.
What happens if you mix the two?

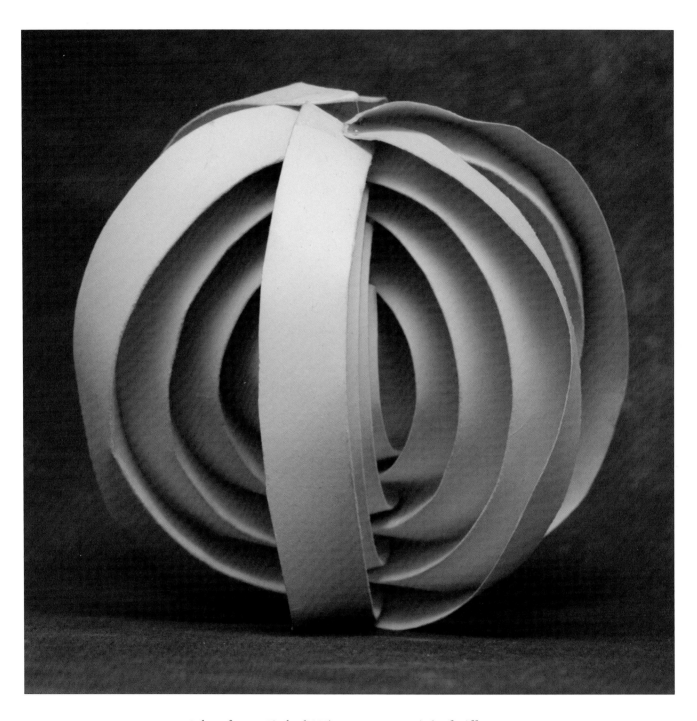

Sphere from a Circle *(2009). From an uncut circle of stiff paper.*

A new idea in origami.

PART IV

INSTRUCTIONS AND DIAGRAMS

The "*Faces*" instructions in this book are geared toward the art student or practicing figure sculptor with a slight acquaintance with origami, but with familiarity representing the human head and experience handling a variety of materials. After the basic technique is mastered, the head can be extended downward to a neck and base by using a longer strip of material and following the simple origami diagrams provided. To vary the effect, alternatives to each of the main facial features are suggested.

The "*Animals*" diagrams are for experienced paper-folders, who should enjoy them. These "pure origami" models are not too difficult, but they are not for beginners. By now there are many good books and Internet resources for learning origami from scratch, as well as origami social groups in many states which are happy to welcome folders at all levels.

The "*Curves*" instructions are meant both for the experienced paper-folder who wants to try something new, and for the art or design student with no origami experience who wants to try something very new.

Good luck to all of you—and happy folding!

Faces

MATERIALS AND TOOLS

- Cutting Surface
- Straight Edge
- Metal L or T
- Matte Knife
- Scissors
- Paper
- Stiff Aluminum Foil
- Spray Adhesive
- Pencil
- Scorer
- Marker

Optimally, the aluminum foil should be thick: 100 microns. This is four or five times thicker than even "extra-heavy-duty" kitchen foil. While kitchen foil can be used, results are far flimsier and much more likely to wrinkle. Foil that's thicker than optimum may be used as well, but it is harder to manipulate. In the United States, a 38-gauge aluminum foil is available from Dick Blick Art Supplies. This is slightly thicker than the optimum, so I recommend not gluing on any paper. Your sculpture will then have a metallic finish instead of a papery one.

For simple projects and experiments, use ordinary brown paper (60 lbs). For longer-lived works, acid-free paper is recommended. Spray adhesives vary widely, so test products carefully before use. Use the strongest brand available. Adhesion should be prompt and full, and not leave areas that will later delaminate. For scoring exposed foil (not the paper side), the optimal tool is a slightly dulled pencil. The graphite glides across the surface better than any scorer. On the paper side, use a dedicated scoring tool. A dry ball-point pen works well.

Most of the techniques in this book will also work with thick pure paper, wet-folded. This takes some practice, since since you can't erase mistakes by scratching, as you can on foil paper. Select a good, 90-lb. (185-gram) watercolor paper such as those by Canson or Fabriano.

PREPARATION

1. Roll out the foil. Most projects require a length of between two and four feet.

2. Spray on the adhesive, taking care to cover the foil completely. Test areas with a finger.

3. Roll out the paper.

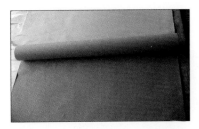

4. Smooth it down with your hand or a spatula.

5. Trim excess.

6. If the project requires it, add a thin colored paper to the opposite side of the foil in the same way, prior to trimming.

HEAD

1. Begin with a rectangle of paper backed with stiff foil about 12-15 inches wide by 20 inches tall for a life-size face.

2. Make two crimps of parallel pleats (MVVM). Fold the lower one first and cover it with the upper one. Each band of the crimp is about a ½ inch (1 to 2 cm) wide. The lowest line is about half-way down the sheet.

3. Raise the upper fold in two locations for the eyes. Distance from eye to edge is about the same as that taken up by the eyes. Note: this move makes the sheet slightly three-dimensional, so folding has to be done in the air, not on a flat surface.

4. Now reach in and pull out the lower eyelids.

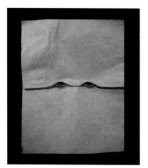

5. Push in the area around the eyes to indicate the eye socket and eyebrow. Firm up the bridge of the nose slightly at the same time.

6. At the edges of the sheet, bend up a little corner of the upper-eyelid flap to form the tops of ears.

7. Now bend down a little corner of the lower flap. This stretches out an ear. Sliding your finger inside the earlobe can make the ear larger.

8. Along vertical lines running just left and right of the eyes, bend the sheet back. Bring the eyes a little closer to each other, sharpening the bridge of the nose.

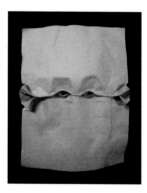

9. Like so.

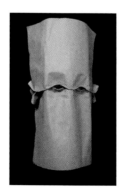

10. Unbend. Make two triangular crimps rising from the bottom of the sheet; the crimps meet at the center line. The apex reaches to about 1½ inches below the eye line. The outer triangle line is a mountain fold; the inner one, which bisects the angle from the apex, is a valley. The angle of the whole assembly at top should be around 90°: more gives you a more protruding nose; less a more feminine one.

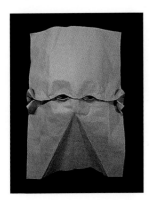

11. After joining the edges, flatten the layers from behind to make a single surface.

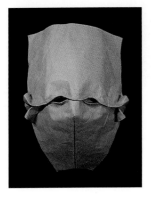

12. Make an indentation about ¾ of an inch (2 cm) under the apex of the nose cone, and about 2 inches (5 cm) wide. Sharpen the nose cone as a whole into a more pyramid shape.

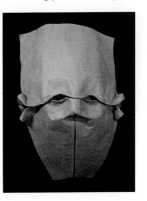

13. On each side of the base of the nose, sink some material slightly under the cheek. This creates a furrow and the line marking the outside of the nostril, while bringing the cheeks slightly closer.

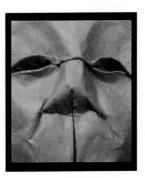

14. Bend back the plane of the face temporarily to see how it looks.

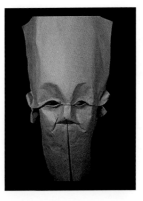

15. For the chin we are going to use the same line and the same method as for the nose. Crimp two triangles (outer mountain fold, inner valley bisector) to the center line. Fold through all layers.

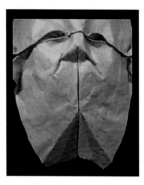

16. Flatten from behind to form a single surface inside.

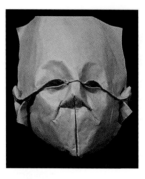

17. Now make a slight indentation for the mouth, about midway between the nose and chin.

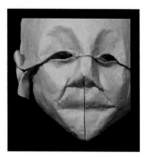

18. Reaching from behind, increase the indentation and close down the lips. Make a second, softer indentation for the bottom lip. Note: if the mouth-line has widened too far, scratch out the excess from in back.

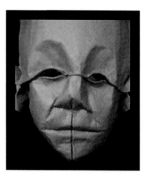

19. To shape the head and hair, insert two triangular crimps that reach from the top of the sheet all the way to the forehead, roughly in line with the eyes.

20. Now close the flaps. The angle between the top of the head and the forehead should be more than 90°; if it isn't, make a smaller-angled triangular crimp.

21. Put another triangular crimp, starting from just over the ears, and reaching the apex about half way to the next line up. This brings the back of the head down a little further, while leaving material in front of the ear to form side locks.

22. Slightly press in the sides of the head in front of the hair.

23. Clean up. Flatten the unused part of the eye-lid crease so it is less prominent. Fix the ears, possibly bending them out so they are more visible. Adjust the join of forehead to hair, sinking the forehead slightly but without creating a harsh fold. Sink the center of the hairline. For a more feminine head, use a longer initial strip to make more hair from, and manipulate steps 19 to 21 so that hair and head rise more steeply from the forehead. If the eyebrows are too high or arched, bring them down. Scratch out all mistakes from in back.

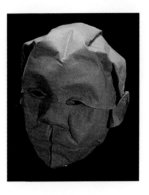

The completed HEAD.

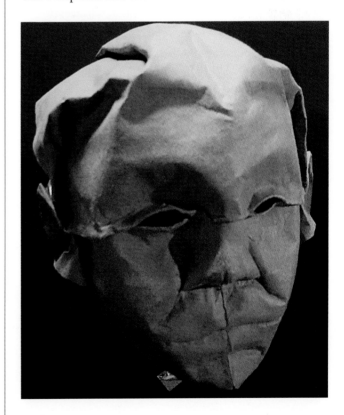

VARIATIONS TO THE BASIC METHOD

These heads and busts were designed within a system, the main objective of which is maximum modularity of features. Ideally it should be possible to choose among very different constructions for the eyes, nose, or hair, etc., without affecting any of the other features. That way variety can be built up and features mixed and matched to meet the needs of a particular project.

HAIR/HEAD TREATMENTS. The initial surface for the hair is always the uninterrupted upper region of the paper strip, reaching to the cut edge; so really it is imagination more than origami that limits what you can do. Ideas can be borrowed from both conventional and sculptural origami. Besides simple crumpling (not shown) exotic cone circles, traditional pleat-folding, curving crimps, spiral tessellations (diagrams in the Curves section on page 96) and drawn waves are among the many possibilities.

EYES

The Basic Method's overlapped double pleat, opened slightly in the right locations, is by far the most direct means of generating eyes. It is simpler to get convincing and symmetrical eyes this way than by sculpting with clay. Following are a few variants you might also want to consider:

1. Bulged out eyeballs (Eric Joisel technique). Press the double pleat out from in back at each eye. Advantage: a rounded eyeball. Disadvantage: the shadow of the eye region is lost.

2. Single crimp over the nose, tilting the forehead forward. Advantage: creates hollows for the eyes without a full transverse pleat. Disadvantages: leaves very little material for eye-detailing and forces redesign of ears.

3. Add a third pleat for an iris. Advantage: Gain an iris. Disadvantage: hard to manipulate.

NOSE AND ITS LINES

The nose forces the most distortion in the face and creates lines that are both non-naturalistic and impossible to avoid. The Basic Method reduces these lines to one allowing the mouth and indirectly the eyes to be formed from that one line.

In the Basic Method, the size and structure of the nose can be controlled by adjusting the acuteness of the cone from which it is made. An easier alternative, and one used

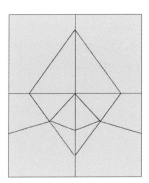 by many designers who work on faces, involves putting in a transverse pleat that cuts from side to side across the sheet. (One such nose crease pattern is shown.) With effort these transverse lines can also be guided downward and hidden under a goatee.

MOUTH

In the Basic Method the mouth is quite shallow, offering little material for detail. Here are some alternatives:

1. Add a second apex to the crimp that forms the nose cone. The new apex should be located a bit below the nose; sink that apex.

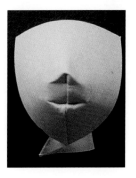

2. The nose cone is made by triangular crimps. These can be bent aside for an open mouth.

EARS AND BACK OF HEAD

In the Basic Method the ears are as far back as the head goes. That is not the physical limit of course, but extending the head farther back this way is costly. Other alternatives are worth exploring too.

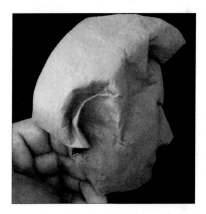

BASE/BUST

By taking a longer initial strip, the head can be extended downward into a neck, and the neck to various busts, bases, or other parts of the body. Diagrams for the Neck and the Shirt are provided on page 76.

HEAD TO NECK

You might want to extend your sculpture downward from the head shown above. If so, here's how you can get a neck that is continuous with it, from a longer initial strip. This is a "regular origami" procedure, so practice it on plain paper before turning to thicker materials.

1. Mark a center line gently, partway up.

2. Mark thirds gently.

3. Mark a horizontal line, gently.

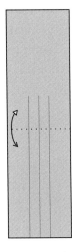

4. Mark 45° lines only to the center line. Turn over.

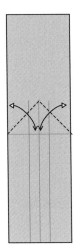

5. Bisect lines just made, bringing them to the center line. This will make the head 3-dimensional.

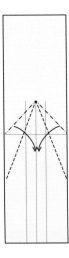

6. Crimp, folding down half or more of the gray area.

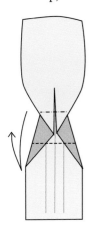

7. Narrow bottom and chin in half, without affecting top.

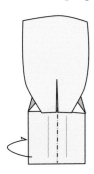

8. Reposition angle of head, so chin sticks out.

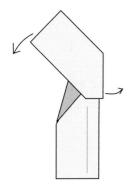

9. Bend neck along third-lines and then round into a cylinder.

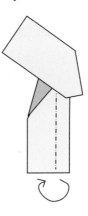

The completed HEAD-to-NECK.

NECK TO SHIRT

This unit is continuous with the Head-to-Neck unit, and is one of several bases or busts that can be used with a head sculpture.

1. On a strip of paper, light side up, mark a square with its diagonals.

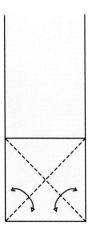

2. Bottom edge to square's center.

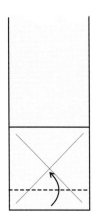

3. Reverse-fold corners. Turn over.

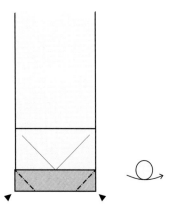

4. Valley fold.

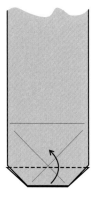

5. Mountain-fold down behind.

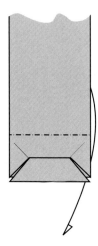

6. Valley-fold, all layers.

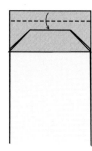

7. Mountain-fold back up. Turn over.

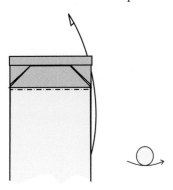

8. Fold one layer, dividing strip into thirds and forming a 45° gusset.

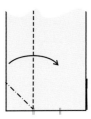

9. Swivel flap around to change its color.

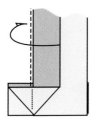

10. Repeat steps 8–9 on the right side.

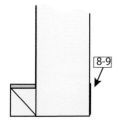

11. Valley fold all layers except for the last triangle. Edges meet at center.

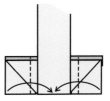

12. Slide collar down until just before the light side shows.

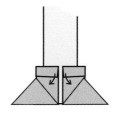

The completed SHIRT with NECK, ready for rounding.

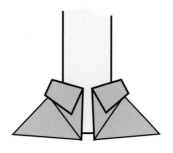

Animals

Most of my origami animals were designed about two decades ago, though many have been refined since then; some are completely new. "Circa 1990" is just when the big surge in technical origami was getting underway, and these models reflect the earlier, more innocent time.

STANDING MAN

(designed 1989, mild revision 2009)

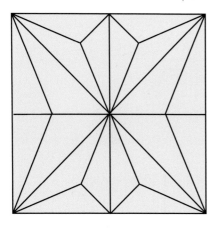

This schematic human figure has a little attitude, and aims to get quickly at its results. Its limbs are put in place promptly in almost the right proportions by means of that interesting hybrid base, the bird-frog base, which has so much potential for other animals too. That base has seven points: since a human body has five (four limbs and a head) two points need to be dealt with somehow. One point gets hidden by a stretch; the other gets turned into a sort of hood.

Two other models pictured in this book are from the same base: the Horse and Rider, and the Heron.

It is hard to believe today, but one actually felt shame at going over 25 steps for an animal model! Efficiency and economy were overarching values then. "Natural referencing" was another ideal which also has become less urgent in much of today's design for complexity.

Begin with a square at least 8 inches (20 cm) wide.

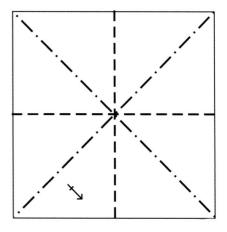

1. Preliminary fold.

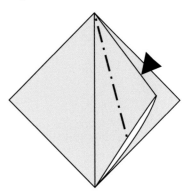

2. Squash one flap. Repeat only on one opposite side.

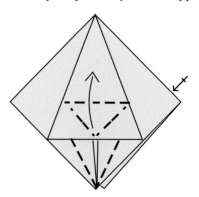

3. Petal-fold. Repeat behind.

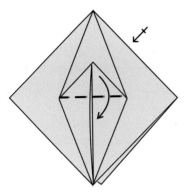

4. Move down small flaps. Repeat behind.

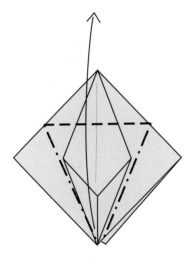

5. Petal-fold through central layer.

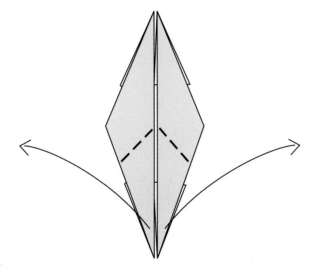

6. The 7-point "Bird-frog" base. Lift and stretch.

7. Valley-fold back down the legs.

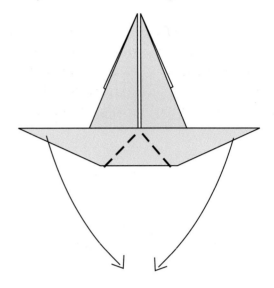

8. Fold down two flaps.

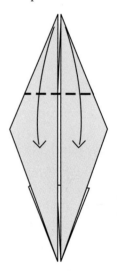

9. Rabbit-ear tip. Valley-fold arms out, from juncture in shoulder blades. Turn over.

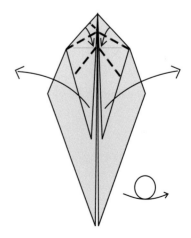

10. Crimp.

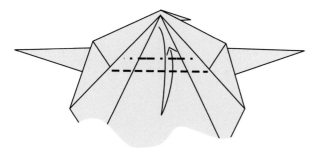

11. Undo crimp.

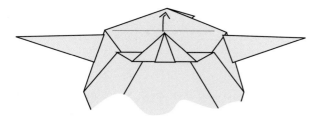

12. Pull apart edges and squash tip.

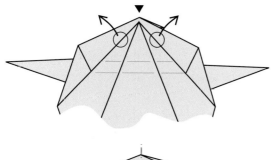

13. Using the crimp lines from Step 10, readjust squash-area to make face more rectangular. (Tip: stick thumbs in pockets next to face, and bend whole model through the middle.) Don't flatten entirely.

14. Valley-fold all layers except the arms along the thickness of the paper (sides of "jacket" overlap).

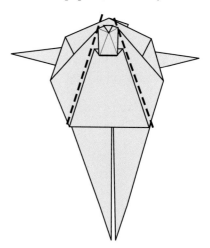

Then curl the "hood" around the head.

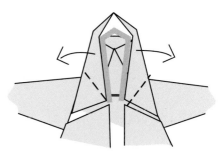

15. Mountain-fold sides, for instant weight reduction. Bring one arm down with a valley-fold.

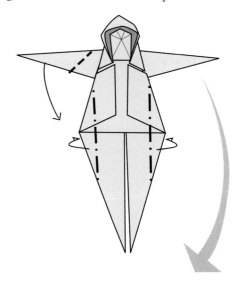

16. Squash hand down, then valley-fold up.

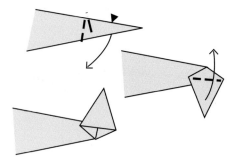

17. Inside-reverse feet. Then mountain-fold leg from inside of knee to top of foot. Leave this fold half open while swiveling the foot forward.

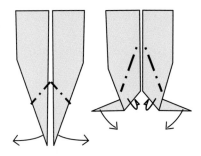

The completed STANDING MAN.

CATS

(designed 1990)

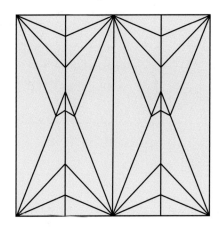

The basic problem of animal origami is how to get from a square, which has four points, to an animal, which has six, in the most expeditious and elegant manner. It's a problem that's been solved many times over the years, a bit differently by each designer.

My solution here was to take and narrow three points in the north and three in the south of the square (the corners and two midpoints). That yields a base which is exactly the same shape and size relative to the square as the bird base, but has six points to the bird base's five.

The trouble with this solution is that proportions end up wrong for most animals. Limbs are short and the body is long. I addressed this here by putting the cats in a stretching posture (which elongates their bodies), by including some reverse folds (which eat up some of the body material), and by extending the limbs "virtually" (which makes them seem longer than they are). But the fundamental design logic is sound, and it was reused in the Horse a few years later. There a more sensible solution to the problem of proportions was found, as you will see.

A variant of this base is used also in the Vase of Gladioli.

Use a 10-inch (25 cm) square, black on one side.

1. Cabinet fold, color side out.

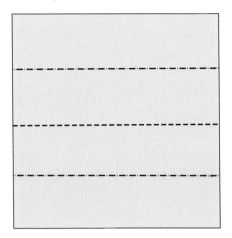

2. Bisect one corner.

3. Bisect that corner again. Unfold.

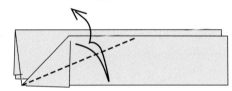

4. Reverse fold 3 times back-and-forth, starting with the longest line.

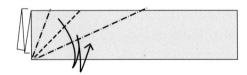

5. Repeat behind, and then with the other corners. At the intersection, make a closed triangular sink (sink direction/layering do not matter.)

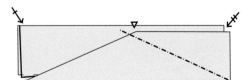

6. Pause to admire the base you have made. It is the same shape and size relative to the square as the Bird Base, but has 6 points, compared to the Bird Base's 5.

7. Valley-fold back one flap. This will be the head.

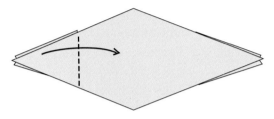

8. Rabbit-ear head forward while mountain-folding the body.

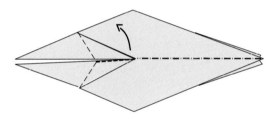

9. Inside the head are two layers. Pull both of them out.

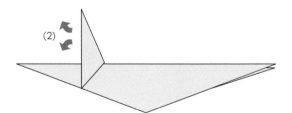

10. Close-up on the head. Grab the front legs and slide the head back slightly. This repositions the head-material slightly next to the legs.

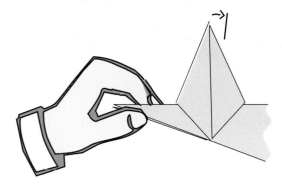

11. Valley fold both sides of the head back along the seam.

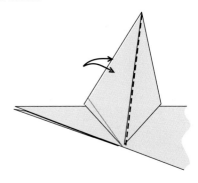

12. Now back the other way. The "chin" now rises slightly from the body.

13. Inside reverse the head, using the chin as reference.

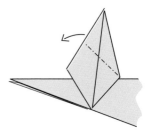

14. Valley-fold open one side.

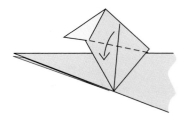

15. If you followed the instructions in step 9, gussets will appear atop the now diamond-shaped head. Open the gussets while valley-folding back, ear to ear.

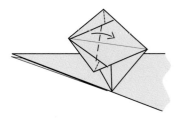

16. Valley fold forward the tip just moved. Mountain-fold the other corners.

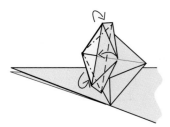

17. The head is done for now. Close it with a valley fold.

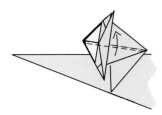

18. Inside reverse all layers, using the tip of the belly as reference.

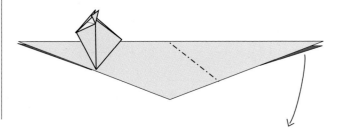

19. Crimp at AC and AB. Point A is midway between D and E; line AC is parallel to line DF. Repeat behind.

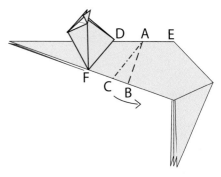

20. Narrow the front legs with a valley-fold. Angle should roughly trisect the leg. Repeat behind.

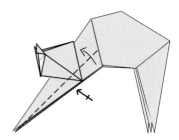

21. Tuck the belly under itself, locking the model. Repeat behind. Bring the tail all the way up.

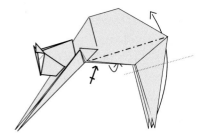

22. Narrow the hind leg (crease does not go to corner). Repeat behind.

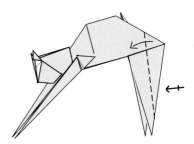

23. Side and rear view. Reverse fold the tail back out, as far back as it will go.

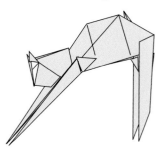

24. Inside-reverse the tail upward.

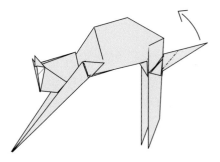

25. Narrow the tail with a valley-fold on each side.

26. Close the tail assembly with an outside-reverse fold.

18. Now for the other cat. Beginning with step 18, outside reverse through all layers.

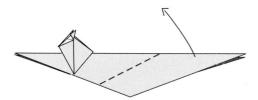

19. Outside reverse down, again through all layers.

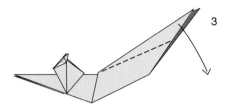

20. Outside reverse the tail only.

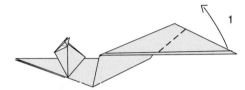

21. Crimp the tail (inside and outside reverse), inside reverse the hind legs, and narrow the front legs, trisecting the angle.

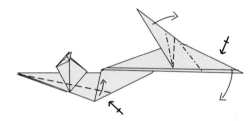

The completed CATS.

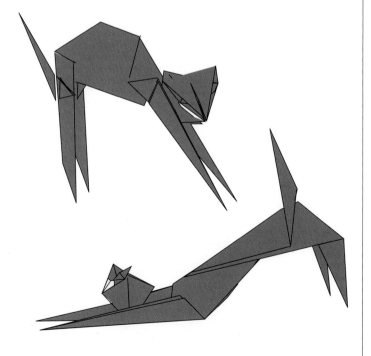

CHAMELEON

(designed 1993)

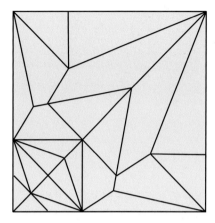

I had a pet chameleon as a boy, and this is my little homage to it.

I wanted a Chameleon that was just schematic enough. Nothing too flashy for a creature that sits on a branch and tries not to be noticed! Of course if what you really want is a Chameleon with horns, split feet, grasping limbs, and a long pink tongue laying hold of a full-featured cricket, all from one paper square—well, no one is stopping you.

This model includes a move in the middle of the fold-sequence that is not common in origami. The dorsal ridge gets raised, and then settles in one position only. While this is a completely geometric fold, the correct position is found by feeling the paper, rather than visually or by an alignment fold.

There are a few other lizards hiding within this same Chameleon structure, and with minor variations in the later stages (playing with the ridge, or color-changing the belly) you can discover for yourself an Iguana, Collared Lizard, Casquehead Lizard, and so on.

Begin with a square 8 inches (20 cm) wide, color side up.

1. Fish base.

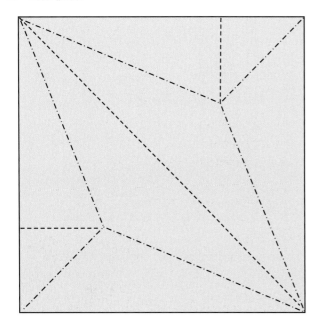

2. Fold and unfold, corner to fin.

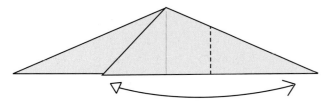

3. Fold and unfold, aligning mark from (2) with edge.

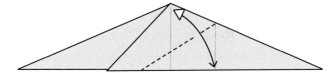

4. Inside reverse up.

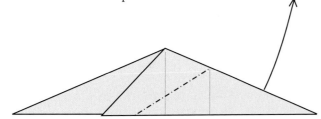

5. Open.

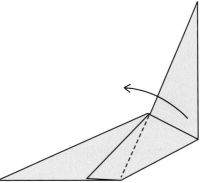

6. "Un-petal-fold."

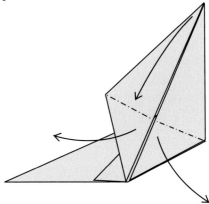

7. Valley fold corner to line.

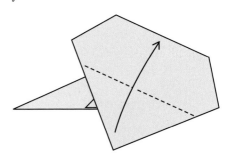

8. Close, while crimping central area.

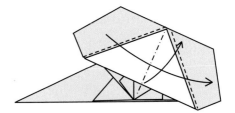

9. Valley-fold open one flap.

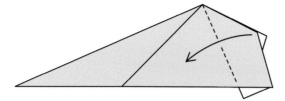

10. Mark the angle bisector.

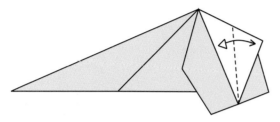

11. Inside -reverse corner while bringing the tip forward.

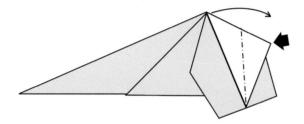

12. Crimp, tucking some material under. Top of triangle (head) continues line of the body.

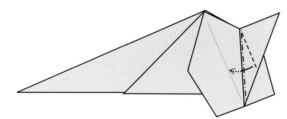

13. Close back flap.

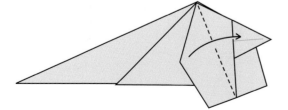

14. Looks like this. Open slightly from on top.

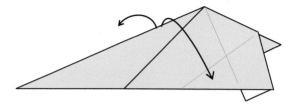

15. Raise point at top of head, while sliding thumb back to the end of the tail, to raise a "dorsal-ridge." Model won't close.

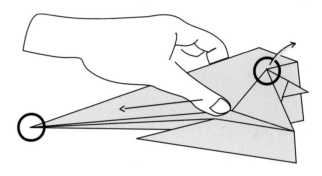

16. Close the model anyway, working from the tail inward, and wrapping some of the front of the ridge around the head (feel for the bulge underneath). This is a geometric fold—there is one place for the ridge to go.

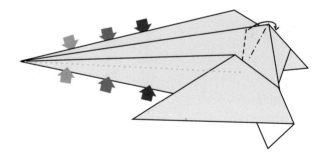

17. Looks like this.

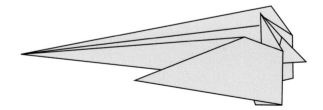

18. Open again, and reposition (sink) the crimp under the head to restore symmetry.

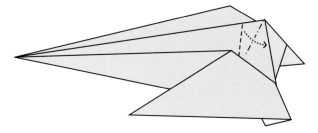

19. Valley-fold fin forward, using the intersection of the lines as a reference. Repeat behind.

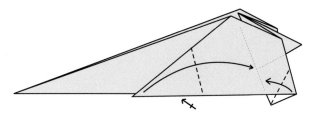

20. Narrow the tail with a mountain-fold, tucking under on both sides. This move narrows the front legs too.

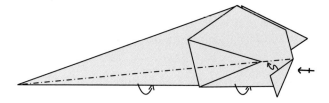

21. Narrow the front legs, tucking the flap into the pocket underneath. Bring down the hind legs slightly. (Note: if you want the hind-legs to be independent, pull them all the way down then push them back up, freeing material at the join with the body.)

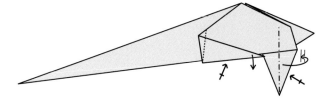

22. Outside-reverse the tail. It will not be symmetrical.

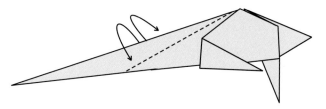

23. Inside-reverse the tail. Tuck the tips at top of body inward, both sides. Crimp the front legs forward. Narrow the nose slightly.

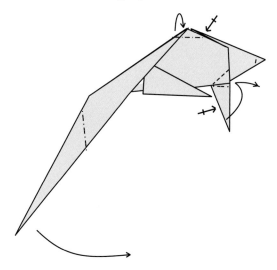

24. Crimp the tail (no need to sink layers), spiraling it inward. Tuck bottom of head inward, narrowing it.

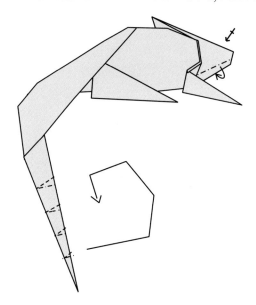

25. Reach into the pocket, and pull out material for an eye. Fold it as a small cone to make it protrude. Repeat behind.

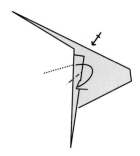

The completed CHAMELEON.

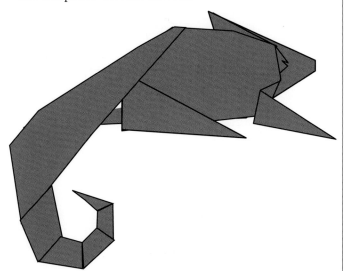

HORSES (STANDING/GRAZING)

(designed 1993, many modifications over the years)

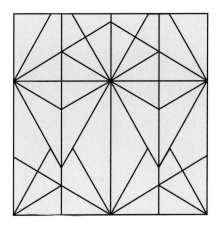

When this was first invented there weren't so many good horses in origami. Now it's getting pretty crowded at the finish line.

Out of sheer boredom I decided that the main division of the square should be into thirds, rather than halves, and that the main angles should also be thirds of corners—30°—rather than the usual power-of-two divisions. Like Dave Brill, I have a special fondness for the underused 30° angle.

A strange thing happened during the evolution of this design. For almost a dozen years I had stopped doing origami, and during that period standards toughened: open-backed animals came to be seen as inferior to closed backed ones. Today this horse has a closed back (though an open head), but in its 1993 version the back was open. What I discovered when I returned to origami was that the old crease pattern could still be used! All that was needed to convert the model from open- to closed-back was to invert a few of the crease assignments. Some of this transformation is preserved in the folding sequence, and you will see it as you fold. ("Ontogeny recapitulates phylogeny.")

This horse stands proudly with an erect head, but a simple modification allows the neck to swoop down and the head to hinge. So essentially the same model can serve for a Standing and a Grazing Horse—and for all postures in between.

This is an "advanced" model. That doesn't mean it takes 70 or 100 steps to make, but rather that in its 40-or-so steps it gets to results usually reached only with longer sequences. The advance here is in the steps that are left out.

Use a monochrome sheet or the head will come out a different color. A 20-foot square yields a life-size horse.

1. Accordion pleat; unfold.

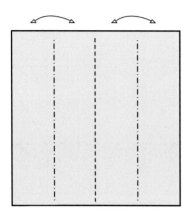

2. Corners to centerline, creating 30° angles. Crease only to intersection.

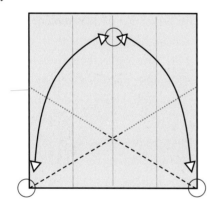

3. Corner to third line at edge, Mark only at intersection (does not meet triangle). Turn over.

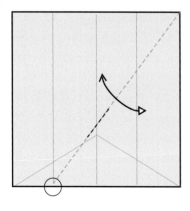

4. Fold to the mark, trisecting the sheet.

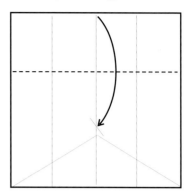

5. Form 60° angles through both layers. Turn over.

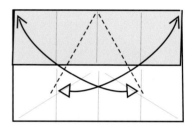

6. Accordion pleat, color side out.

7. Mark at center only, folding down from top. Repeat behind.

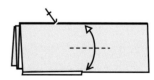

8. Inside reverse all layers of thick end along existing crease.

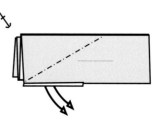

9. Inside reverse triangles.

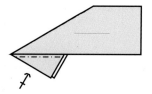

10. Results. Open back to Step 6.

11. Bring flap to front.

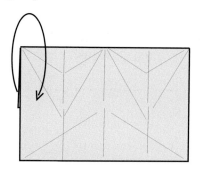

12. Fold white corners along existing creases.

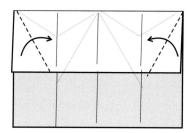

13. Fold over itself. There will be an overlap.

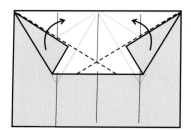

14. Results.

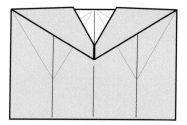

15a. Accordion pleat, while collapsing equilateral triangles and raising center tip forward.

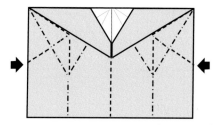

15b and c. Top and side views during collapse. Fins swivel around and up.

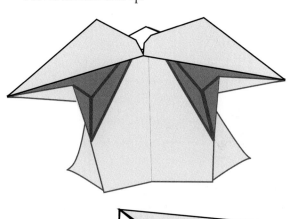

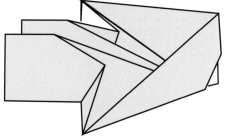

16. Fold down triangular flaps. Repeat behind.

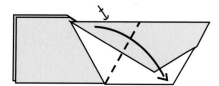

17. Rabbit-ear down. Repeat behind

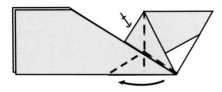

18. Release material under rabbit-ear. Lift and raise, both sides. WARNING! Open model slightly before inverting tip, or it will tear.

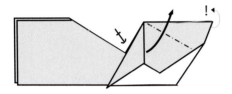

19. Petal fold along crease formed in step 2. Repeat behind.

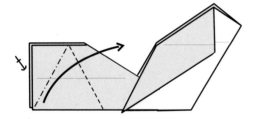

20. Open top and swivel entire model around its base. Valley-fold at bottom becomes mountain-fold, no other new creases are formed. Open back becomes closed-back.

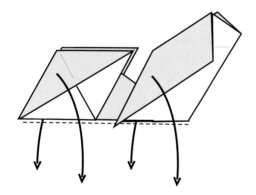

21. Tuck under small triangle of material in front, and valley fold up shallow triangle at rear. Repeat behind.

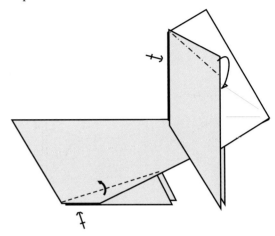

22. Narrow rear legs and tail, both sides. Open-sink white front. Bottom of triangular sink should point down.

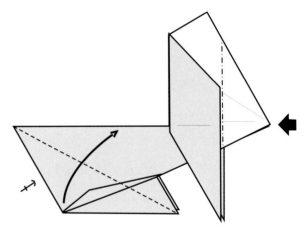

23. Tuck belly under, using creases made in step 7. Repeat behind.

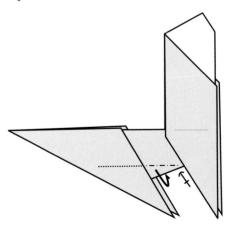

24. Tuck front of belly a little further (no reference).

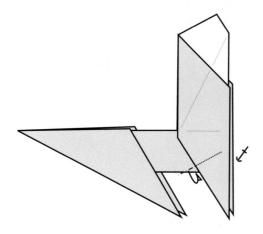

25. Results.

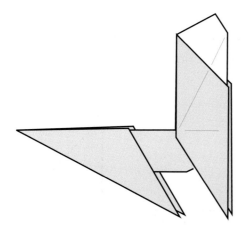

26. Valley fold one side. White tip will curl forward.

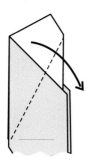

27. Rabbit ear to form head and ear, using the color shift as guide. Repeat steps 26-27 on other side.

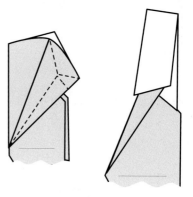

28. Double-rabbit-ear, bisecting the leg and neck. Undo.

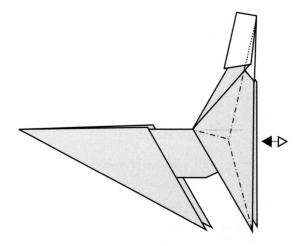

29. Crimp along creases, then restore tuck.

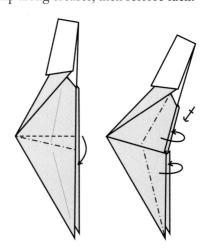

30. Crimp and bend down neck. Raise mane.

31. Double-rabbit ear hindquarters. Tail angle is bisected; legs are trisected.

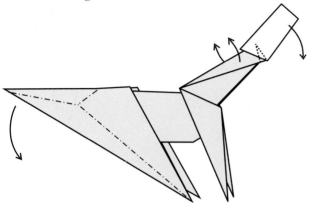

32. Outside reverse hindleg through all layers. Reference is the body layer just underneath. Pinch and narrow forelegs.

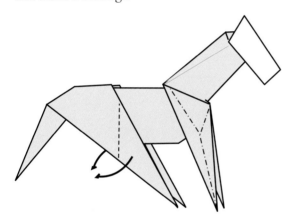

33. Sink hindlegs.

34. Inside reverse legs, outside-reverse tail.

35. Pull tail apart near tip, squaring it.

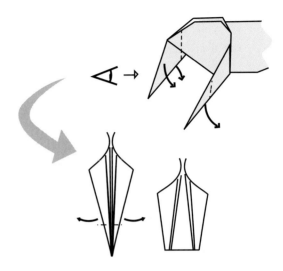

36-40. Clean-ups. Pinch the ears. Round the body from the bottom. Peel some of the mane off near the body; mane should form an arc. Pull some upper-leg material out to form a chest.

The completed HORSE

Now for the Grazing Horse. Make a complete Standing Horse, then take front apart to step 28.

41. Double-rabbit-ear front, bringing neck forward and down, while rotating whole assembly around body (sort of an outside reverse).

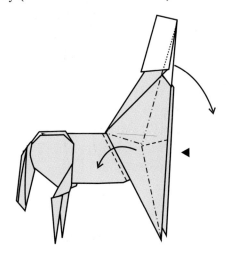

42. Narrow neck, bringing head all the way down. Adjust leg position.

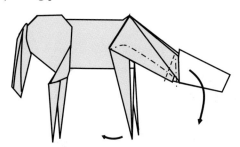

43. Munch on grass.

The completed GRAZING HORSE

Curves

MATERIALS, TOOLS AND PREPARATION

For the curve folds, you have three choices of material:

- Pure Paper (thick stock)

- Paper plus Foil (prepared as in the "Faces" section)

- Polypropylene

For freehand curve-fold tessellations, use a foil plus paper combination as described in the Faces section on page 66. (Foil in a wider thickness range—50 to 150 microns—may also be used.) Score curves on the foil side with a pencil and on the paper side with a scoring device. After scoring, arc the whole surface and begin reinforcing your creases one by one.

For curves that will be scored mechanically based on computer input, use paper or polypropylene.

For concentric circle models, use either thick paper or polypropylene. Prepare a circle guide as described below. You will need a pencil, ruler, hammer, nail, scissors, and a strip of card stock.

HOW TO FOLD CONCENTRIC CIRCLES

First make and use your own circle guide.

1. Take a strip of card stock, 1 inch wide and 1 foot long (2.5 x 36 cm). Mark a long center line with a pencil.

2. Mark off 1 inch (2 or 2.5 cm) intervals on the centerline—ten or eleven of them.

3. Using a thin nail, punch holes through all the intersections.

4. Drive the nail through the zero-point of the guide, through the middle of the paper to be scored, and securely into the cutting surface.

5. Use the scorer to score circles. Press firmly but do not tear the sheet. You can score both mountain and valley folds on the same side.

6. Trim the outer circle with a scissor. This must be done carefully as mistakes are highly visible.

For all models based on full concentric folds, including those that incorporate straight folds, it is best to score and fold the circles completely *first* before introducing any other scorings to the sheet. (Light pencil markings are acceptable.) Once the circles are folded, flatten the paper back down and do any other scoring needed.

FOLD THE CIRCLE

Circle folding can't be done on a tabletop: the paper immediately and everywhere stops being flat. Standing is the best way to do it. A ten-circle pattern can take 20 to 30 minutes to fold.

After scoring:

1. Stand and hold the disk. Flex the paper disk into an arc, parallel to the arc of your torso.

2. With the palm of one hand facing outward, press the first outer crease inward with your fingertips to form a groove. Keep your hand stationary and feed the disk to it with your other hand, till the groove is extended all around.

3. Turn the sheet over and do the same with the next circle in.

4. Continue till all the circles are done.

5. Be sure when forming the grooves that creases form only along the scored circles and nowhere else. This takes practice!

SQUARE-GRID SPIRALS

1. Mark a square grid lightly with a pencil.

2. On the center of each square, score a vaguely swastika-like curve.

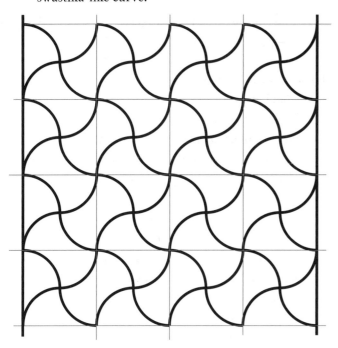

3. Turn over, and score a rotated form of the same

4. To collapse, arc the whole surface, indent one area at a time and gradually sharpen all creases. For an interesting variation, try repeats with inversion.

TRIANGULAR-GRID SPIRALS

Same idea as with the Square-Grid Spirals, only this time use a triangular grid. There's an interesting difference in the resultant pattern.

You can also try this with a hexagonal grid.

CONCENTRIC WINDER

1. Fold concentric circles on a smooth disk.

2. Flatten, and cut a radius.

3. Overlap one side on the other. Wind up.

Tip: To untighten an overly-wound Winder, pull the surfaces apart vertically a little first.

SPHERE-FROM-A-CIRCLE

1. Mark 8 diameters lightly with a pencil.

2. Score the circles.

3. Cut out central circle.

4. Flatten and score the zigzags

5. Fold into sphere.

6. Secure with pins.

Note: This can be done with any number of diameters, but size decreases proportionately.

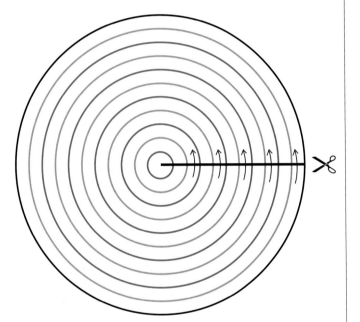

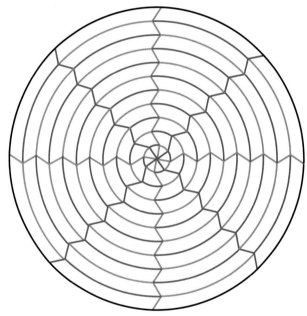

About the Author

Born in Boston, Massachusetts, Dr. Saadya Sternberg grew up in both the United States and Israel and has lived and worked in Paris, London, and Budapest. Today he resides in Beersheva, in Israel's Negev. He studied painting and sculpture at an early age from private teachers, then went on for formal training in aesthetics and philosophy at Harvard and the University of Chicago. He has taught philosophy, art, and biology at universities in Israel and abroad.

His origami career began at age 12, when, hospitalized in Jerusalem for an illness, he was given the origami books of Robert Harbin and Samuel Randlett. He joined the Chicago Area Origami Society (CHAOS) in 1987, the same year it was formed, and later served as its publisher. At that time he began producing novel animal designs, and he began his explorations of face-making from folded and crumpled foils.

He exhibits his origami and other fine art in museums and galleries in Israel and around the world. In 2007 he curated the first large-scale international exhibition of paper-folding in Israel: the well-attended "Treasures of Origami Art," at Haifa's Tikotin Museum of Japanese Art. He regularly speaks, writes, and publishes on origami, art, science, and their relations.

Bonus DVD

Formatted for play on home computers, this special DVD will take you
inside Saadya Sternberg's studio in Beersheva, Israel. You'll join Saadya
as he creates several pieces for three different types of origami sculptures:
faces, curves, and animals. Saadya patiently takes you through every step
of the process, showing you how to create your own sculptural origami.
You'll feel as though you are in the studio with him!